SIGNAL::NOISE

Also by Miriam Goodman

Permanent Wave

SIGNAL::NOISE

poems by
Miriam Goodman

The ratio ($\vdots$) of signal-to-noise determines
the clarity of sound as it comes over a wire.

5/83 Allen 12.95

ACKNOWLEDGEMENTS

Some of these poems have been published, in slightly different form, by the following magazines and anthologies: Shankpainter ("China and Silver," "Computer Lab," "Burrow," "Figure/Ground"), Aspect Magazine ("Trespass," "Staircase," "Industrial Park from the Air"), Word Guild Magazine ("Job Hunting," "On Wishing to Avoid the Bill"), Dark Horse ("Spring in the Industrial Park," "Cheating on Company Time," "Going Concern"), The Real Paper ("Vinebrook Plaza Demolition," "The Women Study in Workshop Together"), Radical America ("Cafeteria"), Niagara ("Reviewing the Possibilities"), Arion's Dolphin ("Signal-to-Noise"), Tendril ("Longing") and Inside The Mirror Pomegranate Editions ("Morning, Swan's Island," "Celebration with Geraniums").

Photographs by Jamieson Hess
Book Design by Donald Krueger
Typeset by dnh Typesetting, Inc.
Paste-up by Don Leamy

Thanks to Ruth Goodman for typesetting this book, and to these friends who read the manuscript and gave their suggestions: Robin Becker, Celia Gilbert, Suzanne Berger, Naomi Chase, Marcia Lieberman, Leslie Lawrence and Shane Snowdon.

Thanks, also, to The Ragdale Foundation, Jane Kogan, The Ossabaw Island Project and The MacDowell Colony for providing residencies during which many of these poems were written.

Library of Congress Catalogue Card Number 82-71819
ISBN 0-914086-39-1

The publication of this book was assisted by a grant from the Massachusetts Council for the Arts and Humanities.

Alice James Books are published by
Alice James Poetry Cooperative, Inc.

ALICE JAMES BOOKS
138 Mt. Auburn Street
Cambridge, Massachusetts 02138

This book is for my cousins: Sue Haven, Danny Perkis, Harry Blum, Marty Gross, Lew Perkiss, Lester Blum and Bob Perkis. Their kindness to me is gratefully acknowledged.

CONTENTS

I

II

III

I

JOB HUNTING

A sign at the end of the street says STOP, so should I?
A truck draws a sound from the road: day overcoming
its inertia. The air is a light shawl, fragrant
with clover. Someone in every house has cut
the weeds along the curb. Someone in every house
is sleeping. I rise, subside indecisive, as if
I hadn't known this city.

It's a settled life I seek to move back into: behind desks,
behind dashboards, carried by the wheel of habit.
The sun in the wheel of the sky and the horizon make
a different axis, set the thaw streaming,
warmth from rocks. I fall quickly to despair,
a mired stone. Who knows if I may return, or when?
Whether these stones litter, or take the sun?

GOING CONCERN

Seeing how the ribbons of hysteria
twist and climb and reappear
who wouldn't take a job?

Who wouldn't grab the towrope
of ambition, ride along behind
the corporation, out of the murk
of chaos, private griefs?

Except there are some plans
you cannot live with. For instance,
here it's pre-cast concrete
architecture. Here the architect
made many rows of windows, but
the sun is in our eyes all afternoon.

Who lets the light in and
forgets to put up sunscreens?
Who wants to look at glare
without a shade?
Now we look like tent city—
the windows hung with colored cloth
we brought from home—or like Brasilia
with the washing on the line.

We could be fired; it could be formalized:
dismissal by the President for spoiling his facade.
Still for now I have the corporate
umbrella, the fellowship and the enterprise:
praise God.

COMPUTER LAB

How do the programmers look when they work?
Some sit for hours and the room is full of noise.
Keyboards clack. Behind concentric grillwork—
whirring fans. Hammers knock the print heads
on the teletypes. And under the assault, the programmers
slide down in their chairs like paper in the platen.
Chins on chests. A desultory finger lifts and strikes
a key. The image on the cathode-ray-tube changes.
Bluish light. The disconnected dots construct a message.
Dry and steady, thought pays out like rope.
They breathe, they shift their weight, they tilt
their heads, they flex their feet. So silent
are the programmers, sitting under fountains
of white noise.

CHEATING ON COMPANY TIME

Since we are miserly with time,
our appetite is scheduled: adultery
or lunch. Every working hour,
leave accrues: a month's vacation
in a well of years. Who plays the numbers?
We do, sign the promissory
notes. We fill out time cards
for our dance with guilt. We say
we're out to lunch and come back late,
a pretext for our assignations.
At 2 and 3 and 4 we're waltzing in,
resolutions broken, picturing
a phantom at the desk, where,
had we stayed, we would be still
and real and admirably working.

VINEBROOK PLAZA DEMOLITION

Before the river froze, we went canoeing,
saw a paddling of ducks and drifted alongside.
All I thought of was commuters, lanes
that run in parallel, drivers glancing
at each other. Now in traffic, I
recall the river. I pass the demolition.
My head turns stiffly in its collar.

I think of how the plaza rose from swells
of marsh, the buildings used before completion.
Lighted windows made a row of portraits—
salesmen signing contracts in their shirtsleeves.
Today I see it go to nothing. Blinds
are flung over the sills like quilts to air.
They have unbuilt it from the inside.

A little yellow bulldozer navigates the blacktop
like an ostrich. Walls go and a stairway is
exposed, a fretwork lit by sky and sunlight.
The stair converges when I pass it in the car.
The view is eaten and replaced
with rubble. Why should the stairway beg
for climbing as the building's coming down?

FIGURE/GROUND

On the way to meet you
I remember dreaming
I had introduced you
formally, around. I think
of love and praise our love
of lunching. I'm going
through the motions of last fall,
driving the same road
to the same restaurant. The fields
are stuck with snow instead
of corn. Stacks of baskets
are inverted for the season.
The plane of life we pictured,
like the picture plane, retreats. Our old
affection shows like stubble
through the rows. What do we
with our stolen time? We eat.

SECRETARY

Her desk creates a harbor in the hall.
Without a cubicle to hide in, she's approachable
like land on the horizon. Close in,
you see her swivel round, serene, her finger-
nail on HOLD, pale and polished
at the black Selectric.
A bud vase with a rose he gave her.
Every day she brings the lunch her mother packs.

Against the waves of new disorder
she hurls the force of her restraint,
a bulwark when you come at her:
"Have we more envelopes like this one?"
She tells twice like a channel buoy, sounding
a firm keep off: "No, we don't, Miriam.
We have none at the present time.
They've been on order since July."
Her answer keeps you right on course.

HAPPY ENDINGS

1

Anybody see that open-heart thing on TV last night? They
shut down the heart for a couple of hours while they work on
it. I wanted to watch the hockey game but I got interested.

2

I'd like to read these dialing instructions with you.
Transferring a call is the simplest to do: one plunge and it's
transferred. If you can't do it, you may as well throw this card
away. Dial the extension, and say, 'Joe, this is Mary. I'm
transferring a call to you.' When you transfer within the
house, you can say anything you want because the other
person is excluded. You can say, 'This is that jerk who's
always bothering us,' but, when you transfer to the operator,
be careful because the person calling in can hear you. And
speak up if a call has been transferred to you; say, 'Yes, may I
help you?'

3

This is basically the cash cow of the company. As
manufacturing comes on-line we'll be making more and more
of them. As you see, we're continuing to grow. Between June,
July and August, we've added 6 to 8 people. We are expanding,
we are augmenting, we are hiring!

4

Today, the company is sponsoring a buffet lunch for our
employees. What is this all about? A year ago we started on
our product. The prototype took shape last fall and with the
snows of winter, the orders started coming. Our customers in
the industry showed deep interest. And so today we're
thinking bigger. We elevate our sights. This year, every time
you turn around, you'll bump your neighbor with your elbow,
but we know you will put up with it for three more months.
As President, I want to personally express our thanks. We
appreciate your contribution to the product. It's a fine
product. Our shipping rate is up. September was our best
month ever. And now, besides the lunch, I'm pleased to
announce another roving holiday. Enjoy your lunch.

5

When the Company feeds you, you know you're going
to hear some unpalatable news.

6

This change is just a commitment away from that market as
a specific thrust. It's difficult for you technical people to go
with management on this. You've put two to three years of
your lives into the product. To those of you who've put the
time in, we say: well done! Now we ask you, like good soldiers,
to support this decision and go marching on with other
Company efforts.

CONFERENCE ROOM: THE GOLDEN YEARS

Rectilinear furniture;
men and women slump

around a table. How
the ventilator blows.

An artificial skylight;
a man, speaking, writing

in a ledger, the year stamped
in gold on the spine.

XEROX

White page
green bar of light
crossing the miles of the page
like an iron

comes to the end
goes out
don't bring it up again
don't bring it up

apron of light
pertinent, topical,
ON and levitating
works till 5

On the highway,
steady moon,
blinking arrows
here, then blank

turn signals
throbbing on and off
intermittent
red

doing the same thing all the time
the exact same:
following the lights,
light passing in a slit
below the door.

CAFETERIA

Clock up on the wall
eggs us on. We pack
the table for a game
of cards. Electric waxer
works here twice a day
on schedule,
bumping the machines.
In goes a quarter
good as a base hit.
Down falls juice in cans.
Up goes a cheer.
Salt and sugar: free
done up in packets.
Bundled like grains,
we strain at limits.
The machinist who buys coffee
finds me writing, asks
if I am making a report
on the people who buy coffee
in the middle of the afternoon.

STAIRCASE

On the stairs, I think of Hebrew
slaves trudging up the ziggurat
carrying reports instead of stones.

Flood light at the top beams
on my ascent as if the work
I piled up yesterday were bricks.

The first thing to surmount is yesterday
and everyone's "Good morning!"
coming down. Coming down

there's someone on the pay phone at
the bottom, talking low and private
to the wall and I imagine phoning

from the bottom of the well, and the tall
skinny man who comes to change
the light bulb, with his long, long pole.

SIGNAL-TO-NOISE

They were filming the Hitchcock episode where the outline of his profile is drawn on the wall. He must walk up to it and fit it exactly. He keeps failing to do so. They retake the scene. A crunch. Someone has stepped on a flashbulb right at my ear, breaking in, interrupting, and I'm instantly awake, frightened.

God, the roller coaster that goes on the outside of the building and has to jump a gap to get back on the track . . . Like an external spiral staircase, it carries the seated audience outside the building and in again. People change off being in the lead car. They don't like doing this. The ringmaster wants me to go on to divert them. I have some kind of wordy animal act and a partner.

We don't all dress to suit the work we do. I, for example, was in a straitjacket for the cooking-lesson dream. They told me to mix with old vanilla pudding, draw my sleeves through the batter and tie my hands behind me. "Lie down," they said. "You will spread the cake."

II

ACCOMMODATIONS

1

Both who raised me buried now,
both women,
caught in my father's view-finder,
printed under a tree.
It spatters them with shade.
Their shoulders are pulled earthward where they're going.
Mother's knees bend fat in her secretary's stockings.
The table of her lap—my jumping-off place—broad,
her forehead broad, ballooning in my reverie,
the picture of a thinker giving birth.
By then my Aunt was blind. Her hair
looks white in bluish kodacolor.
Back and forth she swung between her sisters,
sweeping up the dirt. Still, my mother was
the one who tired first. Comfortable Mother,
my discovery, you died in your sister's arms
as she made you comfortable.
Now there's nothing I can do for you.

2

At first, I tried to do things as you
taught me: to keep the house, to fill
the house with peace. Our first house
like our vision of ourselves,
left all the spaces open. He brought a banjo
and his chinoiserie. There was an inglenook,
a place for company. Then the babies came.
The house grew difficult to live in,
the rooms, confined. He took the walls down,
made new entrances. I studied dreams.
Mother, what's left to give our daughters
but a habitable trick,
so in a state of sorrow
they have a place to go?

3

You never made up stories, but I tell
this about you: sleep was your refuge. You worked,
came home, changed back out of your dress,
opened the newspaper and fell asleep.
Later in your room, so quiet you could hear
your eyelash blinking on the pillow,
you'd close your eyes on the familiar picture,
let your life grow mysterious.

4

You see, I already know how to live alone.
What's missing is the man I could imagine touching me,
the way he put his fingers in the clay.
I'd like to show this beauty to my daughters.
If I am circumspect, how will they know?
Hunger, like a wrecker's ball,
proceeds against the house
and you reproach me:
What kind of housekeeper
keeps order this way?
Who has let things slide?

5

The black bird blows through the evergreens,
hangs off the branches. Your family's opinion
blew you like a rag. I lived my
first life like your last, afflicted.
Becoming vertical, I am a chair,
but delicate. No one sits in me.
the legs I stand on
have been split into a fanfold
of thin slices. The base of my support
is spread. I send my daughters letters,
strike the keys, observe winter
through a double pane—the brittle armature
of trees, the sky flushed—
hold the carbon of the letter to the light,
see where it's torn at the periods,
the endings an era,
unevenly blue.

ON THE ISLAND

The house we came upon
had burned to the ground.
You climbed down through the cellar hole
where ordinary articles looked strange.
You found a cooking pot, a ladle.
I picked up granite bricks,
touched the dried-out mortar,
wondered how they'd stuck together.
The house, roofed over once
and soundly walled, was back
to being earth.

Wind blew the overhead wires
and shuddered through the water in the bay.
Time was limitless when I played house,
declaring to the bush: YOU BE THE DOOR.
Now time stretches out again
on all sides like the tall grass,
you dig on and I don't mind
the sun is going down.

I remember standing at a row of headstones
not believing, till I saw
the coffin lowered in the grave,
life would fit in such dimensions.
Now I can't believe
love's house won't fall away.
Such spaciousness we'll never live in.
Time will see us give it up:
the spruce woods and the needle carpet,
the island bristling with fir trees,
smaller as the ferry pulls away.

TRIP WIRE

I want something to substantiate the death
but it's all vague
from the puffy face in the coffin
to the thin lip line,
the closed eyes and stiffness . . .
and the gestures I think will make
his absence real—hearing the clods,
touching the corpse,
packing the clothes,
the gestures are new and keep him away.

Just the little skip
my feet do, starts it,
on the stair I haven't climbed
in 30 years,
and my past life calling to console.

The ringing now is far away,
a sighing the dog
lifts his head to catch a hint of.
At home, in another city,
I can mourn.
I dial his number,
hear the strange, recorded girl
repeating her one message
where before there'd been
the ringing, his response.

THE DRIVE

The dead are always at their destination.
They flirt with us trying at the wheel
to keep awake, to keep the car from drifting.
And all the horizontals our eyes take
comfort from—the wires overhead,
the silvery edge far out along the bay—
can turn, turn on us and seem a thread
we'll never catch the end of.
Twilight catapults us forward; we travel
in the tunnel of the wave. The pink cheek
of sunset, the ravelled line of trees—
The eye, caught, admonishes: mistrust yourself.
See where your mind wanders away?
You will defect from loving, fly off
the highway, fall in behind the dead.

INTRUDER

I am afraid because the house is open.
Maybe I'm watched by someone I can't see and
I can't see him since the house is dark.
Perhaps he also has two different eyes.
One of his eyes is alive with feeling, the other,
small like the lips of a scar.
That other eye seems crazy, wandering.
I want the chance to find him on the street away from home;
to be the driver of the car
he'll cross in front of. He isn't unaware;
he's planning how I'll enter,
groping for the light. He likes to watch
the fear come over me. Someone mauled him
when his guard was down, but not again.
I tie a scarf around my throat
and wear dark glasses. I have a scar.
I don't want it to be seen.

CHINA AND SILVER

If there are homes
where china can be saved
for generations
I don't know them.

I arrive at the partly dismantled
house of my college friend
at the finish of her marriage.
She asks what I did with mine.
Mine sits in my father's kitchen
in the cupboard
no longer dusted.

What I have now is a living.
Mother, you hoped I would.
I always will.
If I neglect my daily exercise
may I lose the custody of myself;
may I never return to my children.

I drive the highway with a map
knowing myself from the outside, sternly:
so many miles to get there,
many degrees of distance.
The more divorced I feel,
the more imperious,
yet the wish forms like a swelling
underneath: abandon the car,
get out into the woods
and in the dark October soil
on my hands and knees
dig my way through the leaves to you.

INTERIOR DESIGN

From my chair, I saw the tops of trees like torches wrapped in batting, bowing and rising in the wind. I dreamed about my daughters. They came like white ghosts, unimpressionable as marble, carrying roses into the Cirque D'Hiver.

After they were gone a week, I saw their jeep. It was parked near a stand of human legs which were waving in the wind like stalks of wheat.

"Boy, it pass away pretty good," the tall one said.

"What, what does?"

"The growing season."

"Change diapers?" I asked, trying to remember who wore them. "Go potty?" Being old boys and used to the routine, they climbed obligingly aboard the master bed, turned over and stuck their legs in the air. I had everyone's pants down and one bottom poised over a clean white rectangle, when I heard someone talking on the phone in the kitchen about mergers. One of the fathers had found us. Thank God. It wouldn't be much longer now. He was sitting with his feet up in the lean-back chair, talking and talking, the long white cord trailing behind him. Oh the kids were just grand! So cooperative! One had found some candy in the mattress.

The house was rundown but he left us there. I climbed to the second floor to see if it was tenanted. A woman was sitting on the landing in a folding chair, just outside a shaft of light. She was ill. She had cats and birds and was staying with them, preparing them for death. I asked her name. She talked with difficulty: her tongue was pasted with labels. In the crease of her hand lay a red plastic handle. It kept her thumb and fingers apart like a wedge. Her thumb opposed it but it was stiff and unyielding.

She was going into labor. I took charge of her. I put her in the first room we came to. It had two couches pushed together in the middle of the floor. One had a maple wood back with no cushions. The supports were gone apparently, since it had collapsed on top of the other. The quarters looked terribly makeshift, but we used them. She drew a grey army blanket over her. I put some red pillows under her head and feet. She couldn't drag around another step. Every time I left her she got up again. This time she was sitting on my husband's lap. Her eyes were level with his heart. His scent, heat and presence made an environment. She whispered to his heart, "Let me in." He disappeared.

Then I was alone again, peering between the shade and the window, watching two silhouetted figures coming up the walk. They knocked on the door just as if they were entitled to. I turned on no lights but pressed my face to the glass so they could see it, barricaded the door with my body and mouthed: go away. And then I recognized them. It was Lily on the doorstep, and Philip on the path below, smoking. I was ashamed to have mistrusted them, ashamed to be afraid, but I couldn't yield: "You can't come in," I said, closing myself off to them. "Come back later. In the morning," and went to bed.

LUNCH AT THE DESK WITH THE NEWS

Looking at the fallen dead of Jonestown,
then the clock. The jungle rises and is quelled, as scheduled.
They stared into the Kool-Aid
and believed in their release.
The children cried, being made to drink.
The trees were lush around them like an audience.
Seated in the hush of disbelief,
I lean above the clearing,
my cell tidy as an egg crate.
Every cubicle holds one of us,
someone who is one of us,
working for the company,
swallowing a sandwich,
following the pictures.

HOME SICK

Starlings run along the roof outside Sarah's window just across the alley. We see them when I bring her tea in bed. She says, "There's always starlings on that roof and never pigeons," which makes me think of how it was to be a child, in bed before my parents were, sent to be alone and wanting company, and so inventing it in birds, the stiff stuffed animals and the shapes that everywhere arose, that now arise, coagulate, dissolve in her hoarse cough as I listen for her.

She has spent two days coughing, the lining of her lungs inflamed. She likes her blankets soft, likes to lay her cheek on velvet. The starlings grip the roof tiles with their toes, looking for food between the cracks. The hours of the house mean nothing to them. Anything that towers is a tree. Now Sarah's days are rounds of dreaming, waking. She dreams the upstairs hallway smells of juniper. She sleeps lightly, her sheets becoming wind.

MIAMI BEACH

The man has all his hair. The woman, in the cradle of his
legs, slips out of her sleeves to change. Under the tent of her
shirt, she takes off her bra, hands him the straps of her
bikini. He ties; she rises and unfurls. Her hair is cut short
like a boy's, her belly, flat. She rubs his back with lotion while
he sings, looking out at the sea. She bends to stroke him with
large downward strokes, a mother washing her boy.

On the horizon, a line of ships. By the lifeguard's chair, a
line of gulls spaced evenly as fenceposts. Visitors in pairs
stroll barefoot at the water's edge. Elderly men and women,
leathery brown, dip strainers in the surf for shells. Their
arms are bare as if the sun were kindly, as if their children
loved them and the old flesh worth the care. As if youth and
age were here equivalent, they sieve the sea for treasure. They
sunbathe in the shadow of the white hotels.

THE METHOD

This term, you love your students.
One of them and you are alone in the bath.
You are kneeling at the tub, your hands
gloved in lather.
She's cool as a fish.
Your job is to wash her.
The mounds of her body
rise from the water.
her skin is so smooth, so gleaming:
you touch it as if it were stone.
You begin to enjoy it.
She turns under your hand,
she is the poet, you recognize her.
Her blond hair falls like a flag
and her resistant skin
grows warm where you press it.
She sits up in the tub,
begs you to help her.
You think you'll botch it,
after all, you're not her lover,
but the two of you go forward,
and in the dispassionate, receiving water
she gets heated under your hand,
utters her syllables.

THE WOMEN STUDY IN WORKSHOP TOGETHER

We come faithfully
as if there were a house of study
at the end of a path through the meadow,
a house in the woods,
and we walked from the market
to disburden each other of thought.

We observe the forms with tea,
strain to hear the voice behind the page—
a radio turned low—then speak,
become vicarious players,
knock the silent one, amazed, off her restraint.

She waits to find the courage to proceed
as we would wait for birds to find a feeder;
for who would exhibit herself before another's watchful eye,
enter the axis of another's thought,
be so examined? We tempt the bird
with flowers, fragrant praise.
She has to drop her guard to feed.
Then we work as one, dreaming
the explication of the text—
the wind, the waltzing light,
the work of solitude.
We live like those landless Jews
whose Temple was destroyed,
using the text for fellowship,
studying, studying as the darkness fell.

Wings or the shadow of wings may visit us
and one of us bring back from solitude
a commentary so tightly made that by its light
we recognize our hunger. She looks outward,
a cheek propped on a hand, a hand
on the black table, staring, satisfied
beyond the rim of her life.

III

ANOTHER CHANCE

After the mess is made, after the room is shambles,
in the silence after the fight
when no one is speaking, then
what will you have? Another
chance at being good.
You made a mess, it's been
completed; turning now to
something else you think,
penitent, of reform; of how
you will work, stay the full
day, keep your contract.
You think if anyone approaches,
you'll recoil. You do not think
of haste, the people you'll drive
over, the voices you won't hear.

You leave the rice sticking
to the pot, the whining child,
crumbs from the dinner loaf,
leave work heaped on your desk
and drive to a littered living room
where someone loved you, where,
in the permission of his love,
the cloud of demons left
your shoulder, and you stepped slowly
in his room and sometimes danced.

REVIEWING THE POSSIBILITIES

I think to cover myself—not to hide, no, but
secure a welcome by announcing my arrival in advance.
In the event I don't arrive, the letter will. This
fantasy of the killed life and dancing mail arises
at my typewriter as I take my last turn here, thinking
ahead. I could have an accident and die on the road
like a raccoon. Isn't this improbable, since I am
careful to include it as a possibility? When death
takes me, won't I go silently, without a letter
to herald the occasion?

From my mother, there was no message, only a forced
communication, her voice on the wire, resonant
with the last lies: "Mother, how are you?" "Fine."
An accountant's question. But before that, holding
hands, sitting on her hospital bed, nothing to say
except to celebrate by touch our continued relation.
Then, enthroned upon the place that people die from,
her comment, volunteered: "I've been thinking, all night, of
Rebecca Meit, who died of cancer."

MORNING, SWAN'S ISLAND

Upstairs: you, sleeping.
In this kitchen I keep waiting,
breathing the sunlit leaves.
Where does this watchfulness come from,
this stillness in the presence of color?

The mirror wedged in the window jamb
turned from the trees outside
makes a picture of the room,
the woman reading,
of the yellow canvas chairs and wild flowers
pink and purple on the table.

New leaves press against the glass: new drowsiness.
This day to be created when
you've told me I am loved
and I'm startled whenever I
come into it.

THE CLIMATE OF YOUR PLANS

Now it's fall. We breakfast with the flavor of the past.
This syrup, this sweet stuff of trees, takes me back
to February, back to March, how, daily, the weather warmed
till the sap ran when the trees were opened.
Now we climb, warm with our climax, out of bed.
The balcony obscures our view of garbage dump
and cars. I look at the debris a summer's living
has sloughed off: ribs for the canoe you're going to build,
junk mail on the table, plastic jugs on chairs . . .
Amid this stuff, so loath to disappear,
you hatch your slow sweet schemes. The ample concept
of your life: time for all desire to bear fruit,
for twisted limbs to heal. You don't throw anything
away. I'm comforted. You even make a time
and place for me.

LONGING

I drive too many hours, wait all day.
Raindrops on the windshield
turn flat in the light outside
while the sun outwits the earth
and tethers it. Watch the gauge,
half clock, hood of my desire,
it needles through the miles.
In the dark shaft of dreams,
a red elevator falls
and the face I am caught by
looms again, eyes private.

Clocks pave the surface of my mind
like hexagons, separate tiles
of black and white, although the angles
of the furniture dissolve and touch
when I leave a room. Love
filters sparsely through the stiffness,
the chance escaping with the miles.
As if things stayed put without me,
I arrive, dust, organize and leave.

ON WISHING TO AVOID THE BILL

I'd rather not explain/defend/consider what to say.
Then how to fill time on this trip away from you?
I should record my diet, write down what I ate.
No, instead I'll take your picture out,
pop in a peppermint,
and let the upwelling of tenderness fuel me like a soup.
There you are about to fire the hearth.

Steam from the sugaring pan
curls about your face and your sweatered
trunk is lean as any background tree
and supple. The wood you sawed
is heaped up to your right. Your job
to bare the heartwood, neat, in lengths.
How like a tree you are who climbs
and plants and cuts and taps and burns them.

Your mouth is like a candied lemon slice.
Your teeth as white as sugar or the snow
in the woods behind you. Oh I would rather see
than have the picture, see you making syrup
than predict our falling out,
would rather eat than count
the cost, consume this passion
than account for it.

EPISODES

> "Lily fails to lure rich bachelor Percy Gryce
> into marriage and is forced to continue her
> struggle for financial security."
>   —WGBH Program Guide

1

M. fails to leave off mothering her lover
and is forced to go on cooking for him.

J. fails to clean her room
and is forced to decline a supper invitation.

D. fails to forgive her mother's masochism
and is forced to punish herself.

S. fails to suppress her gloomy nature in her art
and loathes her drawing.

A. fails to convince company president B. to manufacture
his invention and sells himself over the wall to an angel.

2

M. resolves to wait until her lover makes the dinner
and so goes hungry.

J., determined she shall have her way, slams her door
and feels lonely.

D. resolves to look after herself better
and takes up smoking.

S. gives away the hateful drawing and makes another.

A. fails to become an independent tycoon
and is forced to invent the lightbulb.

CELEBRATION WITH GERANIUMS

The taxi never does go straight to the address.

Never mind, we made it into bed.
Geraniums on the sill are stiff, as we were
but the light makes moving pictures on the leaves.
Shadows in the leaflight fanned behind you
before your hair fell like a screen over my eyes.

How quickly love and memory change places:
now I'm elsewhere, trying to bear up.
I think of the electric candles that grew haloes
when I sat in synagogue, playing with the focus
of my eyes as the service bore along.

The afternoon draws on outside the window.
The sky beyond is very blue. A book lies open
on my lap; a sunset flush is on the branches.
Then you break in, a room, burst in my mind.

BURROW

The corridor through the woods
was once a cow lane.
Apartment D-4 was a pasture.
Your dwelling is, for me,
a place where I dig in,
walled off from what's around us.
The present is an enclave in the past
as a clearing was, for Cherokee,
an enclave in the bush.
What will become of us
is like the evidence of history
that litters the woods.
Think of a cow amid
this housing complex.
Put the cow on asphalt
in the parking lot.
We limit where we look
like the cows
that ran the lane to pasture,
their only thought for grazing.

TRESPASS

There was a stiff wind yesterday.
It knocked a carpet of magnolia down,
the leaves so regular, all laid in one direction,
it hardly seemed the work of the wind.
We make an odd and random combination
like any objects blown together.
When I wake here, reproof is coming from the trees.
Keep it a secret   secret   secret   says a bird.

Entering your father's summer house was
breaking in. He treats you like
a boy. You have no key. A shadow
curved over your bed like a hung
sword. I chose his chair. My scent
on it? In the boatyard, we climbed
all over a sailboat on a cradle
for repairs. It had a place in history,
a famous name.

                    I kept thinking,
half-expecting to be caught,
we could resurface our behavior
like the boat. The next time anybody
saw this boat, it would be lifted
from the debris of the yard, repainted,
smooth, aground in a museum.
The next time anybody saw
this boat, we might be any
visitors, behind a purple rope.

SPRING IN THE INDUSTRIAL PARK

You fall silent,
lost to the familiar objects
already turning queer;
track lights swerve along the ceiling,
listings lean against the wall.
Stationary you sit,
wedging your finger in your mouth,
turned around and inward
at a hint of rain.
The air around you thickens
like the brain before a sneeze.
The pressure systems gather.
You notice them.
Mud broods below the city bricks;
glue bubbles from the binding of a seam
and you are yawning, dangerous
and comic as electrons charging
through an integrated circuit.

INDUSTRIAL PARK FROM THE AIR

When I wake up caged in someone's dream or plan, water boiling sounds like surf caged in the coffee pot. Such a lonely sound can happen indoors on the days when the fluorescent lights and company are a dream we dream of joining.

In traffic steaming at the lights, I tumble from my thoughts, stretch, can almost touch the other driver talking to himself, or combing his fingers through his hair. I see his elbow resting on the window, shirtsleeve ruffle in the wind; then we go sailing off as the light changes; bicycles and ski racks, the skeletons of our plans.

Driving past the buildings, I remember how I saw them from the air: as if you could pick them up between your thumb and forefinger and place them in the industrial landscape, just the way they had been cut from colored paper for a planner's map, in his Cartesian dream.

A boy's face, huge, on a billboard, looms over his toy. No one else in the boundless blue room. He sets things right. He sees the highways stretch to their extents, the trees as groundcover, buildings hidden by the bush.

Along the highway, purple loosestrife blazes. The cars, now big and too fast, catch the sun. I come up wide-mouthed on the car in front of me. Someone's automobile dream, someone's spark, someone's road, and in their dream I am the laborer, with my dream floating in the summer trees, pacific, uncontending and unplanned.

ARGUMENT FOR PARTING

Remember your list of bottles from the dump?
I think of how you find a way to quantify—
list the miles you skated,
the towns where we made love.
If things add up, you can be happy.
You cut wood daily and the pile accumulates.
Your days become a history.

By means of dailiness, the over-all
is done. Who will know I broke my daughter's
will or poured the alphabet into her ear?
Who else will know I loved you?
Oh sad arithmetic, my name amounts to nothing.
Would you number it on lists? There were
no witnesses; I improvised.

And I don't marry.
I don't buy land.
I get older by myself.

WAITING

1

Be with me like a good girl.
Stay by me.

Was I always waiting to escape,
tethered to the phone,
thinking on the stair
the imaginary ring I heard
would be you, Father, calling?
You're dead, old man, and
I'm unable to go free.
Waking in the middle of the night,
I quit my bed
and come into a new room
remembering your legacy,
your boxes in my basement
which I don't want to open.
There is nothing more to know
except your history.
Time runs out and there's never enough time.
If I repeat myself, the outcome should come
right. The routine gives the day its rightness.

The recipe is here to say you're right.
It's pleased when you have followed its direction.
The pattern likes it when you give it form.
Her father likes to see himself in miniature.

2

My education has outlived its usefulness.
There is my body which I can't shed.
There is my lover. He stations me
and goes along the sea wall, looking smaller,
for the moment, than a bleached stone.

60

He is my eyes adventuring, the tide
spilling in a pool between the rocks,
but not the ocean. I peer into the distance
for his trouser legs. I wait for him,
not knowing why, imagine him unbalanced, falling,
myself not up to saving him.

3

I give myself advice: be more alone.
Your life will ferry you. Let your breath match
the fall of the ship as the engines churn.
Relax your vigilance;
your life will carry you to wide water.

4

I wake to birdsong volleying like stones
under my wheel. I counted the bumps on the road
last night, the rocks that might unseat me.
My hair was blown against my head, my ears acute
as I bent along the road over the handlebars,
hurrying home before the dark. People waved from cars.
I overtook a father and his daughter
out for a sunset walk, passed a church,
the open door, which said a service
was in progress. All said: safe. Stay!
I wondered what they'd want me for.
Above the meadow grass, a deer's white tail
broke cover as it hurried for new grounds,
and the clouds rolled off,
opening a lid for the moon.

POETRY FROM ALICE JAMES BOOKS